Be A Boss

195 Legitimate Ways to Generate Multiple Streams of Income

By: Latrice Handy Jones

DISCLAIMER:

This book is for informational purposes only. This book is not a "Get Rich Quick" marketing tool. Individual results may vary depending on the efforts put in by the consumer of this information.

This book is dedicated to:

All the inspiring entrepreneurs around the world...

Epigraph

"You can only become accomplished at something you love. Don't make money your goal. Instead pursue the things you love doing and then do them so well that people can't take their eyes off you."
Maya Angelou, African-American author and poet

TABLE OF CONTENTS

Introduction

"I'm so tired of living paycheck to paycheck"

It's a sentiment we all have either heard or said before. It wasn't until I got sick and tired of saying it, that I actually took some action to ensure this wasn't going to be my life's' mantra. My journey started in 1994. My family was growing and my husband and I were barely keeping our heads above water. 94' was the year I purchased my first desktop. This was when dial-up via AOL was a way of life and Google wasn't even heard of yet. I get a kick out of telling the true story of how I was the 5th person in the world to have a Yahoo email account. The sad part of that story is, I didn't take advantage of buying Yahoo stock when they were offering it to us new members for $1. It's a prime example of not taking advantage of the opportunities that are presented to you.

In the upcoming pages, I would like to present you with some opportunities that I personally utilize as sources of extra income. I've done extensive research on everything listed to ensure the validity and integrity of the content. My main objective is to empower you with options to supplement your income. The Ultimate goal is that something on the following pages will resonate with you deeply and you'll be led on a path to financial freedom. Regardless of what path led you here, trust that you are here for a reason. The universe is funny that way. I truly believe that there is something in this E-book that can be beneficial to you. Let this be the year when you finally are sick and tired of being "Sick and tired!"

Income Sources 1 – 195

1. <u>10EQS</u> - 10ESQ occasionally has openings for work from home researchers. Qualifications include great English skills, experience with MS Office, and business experience. The pay is based on the task you complete. The more complex, the higher the pay. You get paid via PayPal or Bank transfer.

2. <u>123RoyaltyFree</u> – Sell you photographs and not only will you get up to 60% of each image sold; you also earn 15% of your referral's subscription or purchase, plus 10% of every image sold by a photographer you refer. Great opportunity for freelance photographers to sell your talent. Also a great place for beginners to get started.

3. <u>2020 Panel</u> - Since 1986, the 20/20 Panel has been doing excellent work in the research field. They offer you the opportunity to participate in focus groups and get paid decent money for doing so. I've personally participated in focus groups and I was promptly paid. Please use: latrice.jones@yahoo.com as your referrer should you decides to join.

4. <u>3PlayMedia</u> – This Company is looking for Transcriptionists / Editors. You can be located anywhere in the US. Must have excellent grammar and spelling, as well as a typing speed of at least 75 wpm. You'll also need a speedy internet connection. Pay ranges from $10 – $30 / hour based depending on your efficiency.

5. <u>Ableto</u> – Become a work at home therapist or behavioral coach for Ableto. Requires phone and/or webcam. They also have positions available for a Concierge Navigator, where you will be the link between the therapist and the client. Most positions are located in New York but there are opportunities for remote positions anywhere in the US.

6. <u>About Face</u> – There are plenty of Mystery Shopper sites out there and to be honest a lot of them are scams. I would recommend you check out the Mystery Shopping Providers Association (<u>MSPA</u>) and research companies if you are unsure of their authenticity. About Face has been in the industry for a while and I am an active member. It is an independent contractor position and you will be required to fill out a W9 form for tax purposes. They also ask for a Photo ID and picture of you in Business attire. They pay once per month by PayPal only.

7. <u>Accounting Dept.</u> – The account Dept. is searching for experienced bookkeepers who are interested in working from home full time. They have Virtual Accounting Specialist positions open and all employees are full-time, W-2 employees with benefits. They sometimes have position open for Virtual Senior Controller, CPA's also.

8. **A Closer Look** – This is another Mystery shopping company with a great track record. They have been in the business for over twenty years and have lots of restaurant and hotel shop opportunities. They have a lot of work available. I get opportunities daily from them. They pay once a month for the shops you've done via paper check.

9. **Aira** – Work at home doing voice chats with the blind and visually impaired to help them complete day to day tasks. The sign up process is pretty straight forward. Once enrolled you will be asked to take a 45 minute test to access your skills. US only. Pay may be around $15 hourly. Very Flexible with hours.

10. **Airbnb** - If you're willing to share your living space you can make some pretty decent money with Airbnb. It's not for everyone, but Airbnb has more to offer than meets the eye. They have several ways you can earn extra income by partnering with them. You can become a **Pro Referrer** where you basically search for properties that would be a good fit for the Airbnb database, sign them up and you'll be paid $300 once they host their first guest. On their **Careers** page they also often have opening for remote translators, contractors, and inspectors so check back often.

11. **Allegis Transcription** – They often has openings for Entry Level Transcriptionists. Anywhere in the US. No prior transcription experience required and you will be trained. Must have minimum 75 WPM typing speed and excellent grammar skills. You'll need a Windows PC with Microsoft Office 10 or higher and a transcription foot pedal. Pay is said to be around $16 / hour.

12. **Allume** – Allume is an online fashion styling service for busy professional women. They are actively seeking Online Fashion Stylist and Customer Service Reps. You can be located anywhere in the US. Must have a quiet workspace with a speedy internet connection. Salary is unknown.

13. **Alorica** – They are looking for Bilingual Customer Support. Anywhere in the US. Minimum 1 year customer service or sales experience required. Must be bilingual in English and Spanish (or other language). Agents average between minimum wage and $10 per hour.

14. **Amazon** – Amazon Regularly hires virtual customer service agents in various states nationwide. They also list other virtual positions under the "Remote" job category. No mention of pay rate but I've heard they have a great compensation package.

15. **Amazon Associates** - If you have a social media following, Webpage, Blog, Etc., you can profit off of Amazon Associates. You Get up to 10% in advertising fees when you promote any amazon product on your platform. They have millions of products so the possibilities are endless. They supply you with all the tools you need to promote and it's all free!!

16. **Amazon Flex** – Delivering packages for Amazon is a great source of income. You are your own boss with lots of flexibility and the pay ranges from $18 to $25 per hr. They have a great App that lets you scan your packages, set your route, and see your pay. Check them out!!

17. **Amazon Sellers Account** - Yet another source of income from America's largest online retailer. Open a sellers account and you determine what you want to sell. I've use this platform to sell used books for years. The possibilities are endless. Amazon notifies you when customers place an order and payment for the balance of your orders (net of Amazon Seller fees) is deposited into your bank account.

18. **American Consumer Opinion** - ACO became an online presence in 1996. They now have several million consumers in their database that get paid for surveys and research projects. They utilize a points system where you earn points for your participation and you can convert the points into cash.

19. **American Express** – They frequently have numerous Virtual positions listed. Anywhere in the US. Travel background strongly preferred. You'll also need a quiet workspace with a speedy, wired internet connection. Salary is unknown.

20. **American Journal Experts** - Aje Hires work from home editors. All contractor positions are remote and can be performed from anywhere in the world. If you're interested in an independent contractor position you should definitely apply.

21. **AMV** – AMV is a Tech startup company that is searching for remote Copywriter / Publicist. Anywhere in the US. Must be fluent in English. Experience in content publishing, PR, SEO, or blogging a plus, but not required. Set your own hours and earning potential is up to $2,500 / week.

22. **Appen** – They are hiring Web Search Evaluators and occasionally other virtual positions. You would provide feedback on search results, ads and web page content. Must have a computer with high speed internet access and/or a smartphone that is less than 3 years old. Strong English writing skills are also a must. Pay will vary depending on the job you're doing for Appen. Search engine evaluators may make around $13 – $15 hourly. They pay monthly via check or direct deposit.

23. **Apple** - has openings for work from home iTunes chat advisors. The position pays well and you are considered an employee. They offer paid training and benefits. The competition is pretty fierce for these positions, so you should do some research on Apple before applying. You also get an Apple computer if you are hired. Open to US.

24. **Art & Logic** – Hires work at home software developers with experience throughout the U.S and Canada. They are only considering developers who are able to regularly work 30 or more billable hours per week. If you have experience in this area this would be a great Independent Contractor opportunity.

25. **Art Fire** - Art fire provides a platform for sellers of artistic goods; handmade goods, fine art, vintage, certain designed items, and more. Similar to Etsy and Ebay, they do charge insertion fees and final sale commission. Check out their site for information on fees.

26. **AskWonder** - Open to US residents except those located in New York, Massachusetts, and California. Clients submit questions that they need answers to, and as a Wonder researcher, you do the searching online to find the best possible resources for answering their questions, and then use those resources to provide detailed answers. Work whenever you want, and get paid via PayPal twice monthly. Active researchers earn over $2,000 per month.

27. **Aspira** – Hiring Remote Call Center Agents. They have openings in several US states. You'll need a quiet workspace, standard phone line, and speedy, wired internet connection. Pay is around $11 – $12 / hour.

28. **BabyCenter** – BabyCenter is occasionally hiring work at home community moderators. They also have Design and Editorial jobs available. These are full-time contract positions so if you have experience in these fields you should check back often.

29. **Baker Street Solutions** - Founded in 2002, Bakers Street pays consumers in exchange for their opinions. I have been a member since they started and although I do not get a lot of survey opportunities from them, I still think they are a solid company and worth the sign up.

30. **Book Scouter** - I'm an avid reader so I always have a ton of books around the house. This company mostly buys and sells textbooks but BeBookScouter is an excellent tool to use to see how much any of your books are worth. All you have to do is enter in your book's ISBN number and they will check over 35 online sources for caparison for you.

31. **Belay Solutions** - Belay has open positions for Virtual Assistants and Virtual Bookkeepers in the US only. Pay rate is not stated but I've only seen good reviews about the company. These are Independent 1099 Contract positions so you'll have a lot of flexibility.

32. **Best Mark** – Become a Best Mark mystery shopper. This company has been featured on Oprah and has a great BBB rating. I'm personally a member and I can vouch for their validity. Great company with plenty of interesting assignments.

33. **Beta Bound** – BetaBound is a free service provided by Centercode that offers you a chance to participate in beta tests. Members have tested products from Logitech, Dell, Apple, T-Mobile, Kodak, Yahoo, and many more! You chose what you want to test and there are always plenty of opportunities listed on the site.

34. **BidaWiz** - If you are an accountants or tax experts, you can supplement your income by becoming a work at home tax instructor/expert for BidaWiz. You can work from anywhere and make some great additional income.

35. **BigStockPhoto** - Attention all Photographers!! Grab your camera and let's make some extra cash. With big stock photo you can pocket up to $3 for every image of yours that is sold. You can make a request for payment at any time once your commissions have reached $30.00

36. **Blogads** - Around since 2002, this network lets you set up ad space on your blog and set your own price. You need at least 30,000 page impressions per month to attract advertisers. You get to accept or reject offers from advertisers so you are always in control. It's a nice source of extra revenue and it's free to join.

37. **Blogger** - If you're ready to start that Blog, you should head on over to Blogger. It's super easy and free. You not only get hundreds of themes to choose from, you can also earn some extra income by utilizing **Google AdSense**. Blogger is the platform I use for my blog **The Daily Dollar** and I love the fact that you can buy your domain name and link it directly to your blog for free.

38. **BloggingPro** - It's a wonderful site, chock full of great gigs and jobs for writers. Nearly all of the jobs posted are for freelancers. Many jobs posted don't require a degree either

39. **Blue Mountain Arts** – founded in 1971, Blue Mountain Arts is a greeting card company that will pay you for your original poetry. They are looking for genuine emotions on topics such as love, friendship, family, missing you, and other real-life subjects. They pay $300 per poem.

40. **Bonanza** - This is another great option for you to set up shop and sell your stuff online. There is zero listing fees and zero setup costs. In 2016, Bonanza beat out eBay and Amazon for the "Best Overall" site. You can sell both brand name items, handcrafted items, and good quality used items. They have a large marketplace and a well-designed website. They have an affiliate program also but I believe there is a fee to join.

41. **Brainfuse** - Brainfuse hires Certified Higher Education Tutors. You must reside in the United States and possess a master's degree or higher. They also require you to have prior teaching or tutoring experience and submit to a background check. You get to choose your own hours. Pay is around $13 / hour.

42. **BuddyTruk** - Available in Los Angeles, Orange County, Austin, and San Marcos, BuddyTruk lets you turn your truck into a moving truck and earn money by providing moving services. Earning potential is up to $40 an hour and it's free to join. If you live in the service areas and own a truck, this is a great opportunity to be your own boss!

43. <u>Bustle</u> - Bustle is searching for Lifestyle Writers and Editors. You can be located anywhere in the US. They cover a vast amount of subjects such as sex / relationships, health, mental health, and astrology. Candidates should have at least 2 years of writing experience. Pay tends to be around $16 / hour.

44. <u>Buzz Back</u> - As a panel member for Buzz Back you will be invited to surveys which cover a wide range of topics. You in return earn rewards that can be cashed out. The min cash out balance is $15 via PayPal or Amazon. They have been around since 2004.

45. <u>BzzAgent</u> - BzzAgent will ask you to share your experiences with people you know — not necessarily with BzzAgent. And you can do this via word of mouth, social media, texting, etc. The send out samples and you test them and share your thoughts on the products via social media.

46. <u>CafePress</u> - Be it graphics design, logo or text, CafePress can help you to market your creative content. Design and sell your creativity on actual merchandise with your own CafePress shop. CafePress has a base price for every product, and you can keep the markup amount.

47. <u>CallSource</u> - They occasionally have remote positions for independent contractors. Your role would be listening to recorded phone calls and scoring them based on the company's criteria. Pay is per call. Jobs are not always available so check back often to see what's posted.

48. <u>Calypso Cards</u> - This Company works with freelance artists, illustrators and ghostwriters. They Pay $50 if your idea is accepted. Other opportunities are listed on their submission page that might be of interest to you. They specialize in humorous cards.

49. <u>CapitalOne</u> - Capital One has numerous work from home openings for customer support, customer care, fraud support, and much more. Search for "Remote" in the keywords to see listings. Salary and job requirements vary by role and location but seem to range from about $23k – $35k per year.

50. <u>Card Cash</u> – Let Card Cash know what gift cards you'd like to sell, and they will make you an offer. You can choose to receive either cash or an Amazon gift code for your sold cards. Your friends and people in your area. Turn unused gift cards into cash.

51. <u>Carenet Wellpoint</u> - They are occasionally hiring experienced RN's with an Associates or better in nursing to do telephone triage from home. Search "work from home" in the keyword box to see if they have any work from home positions open.

52. <u>Caviar</u> - Become an independent Food Delivery driver for Caviar and earn up to $25/hr. You get paid instantly for each delivery via Cash App. You must be 18 or older and pass a background check. They've been around since 2012 and have a great reputation.

53. <u>Clara Labs</u> – Work at home as an email scheduling assistant for Clara Labs. Not always hiring. Position is not always open. I suggest checking back often because it's a great work at home opportunity but the position fills up fast.

54. **ClearVoice** - ClearVoice compensates you in points, whether you qualify for the survey or not, that you can redeem for Amazon gift cards, restaurant gift cards or a Payoneer prepaid debit card that you can use anywhere that takes MasterCard. The minimum cash out is $10, and you can participate in surveys and product testing.

55. **ClickBank** - ClickBank has been in business for over 17yrs. They are a proven leader in the affiliate marketing field and they pay some of the highest commissions out there. They are also the largest marketplace you can find on eBooks and other digital products. You choose what products you want to promote and many of the products available on ClickBank will net you reoccurring commission.

56. **Clickworker** - Clickworker offers many ways for you to make a profit off their platform. Creation of texts, Data categorization, Copy editing, Proofreading, Web research, Surveys, Photography, and App testing to name a few. Choose the jobs you prefer and you can get paid weekly or monthly payment via SEPA or PayPal

57. **Clixsense** - Another Paid to click site that offers both cash and prizes. Their member's area is quite busy with offers like paid surveys, cash offers, simple tasks, and games. They also have an affiliate program which is always a plus.

58. **Commission Junction** - CJ has a huge network with hundreds of offers available in every category you can imagine. I like working with them because I control what I want to offer to my audience. You will also get offers from advertisers that want you to promote their product or services. They payout once you reach a minimum of $50.

59. **Conduent** - They are hiring for Customer Care Associates. Most US states. Applicants must have at least 6 months of prior customer service experience. You'll also need a speedy internet connection and a quiet workspace. Pay starts at $12 / hour + benefits and bumps up to $13 after 90 days. Must type "Remote" for Keyword for results.

60. **Confero** - They have a need for shoppers in every US state and also Canada. They were founded in 1986 and are a leading provider of customer experience research services to leading national brands. They pay monthly via PayPal. You can expect to earn between $25 and $45 per shop.

61. **Consumer Press** – This site needs people to write about products, stores, consumer topics, etc. and in return they give Adsense revenue share, Exposure, Education, A Byline, Stats, and much more!

62. **Contemporary Virtual Assistance** - Occasionally has an opening for virtual assistants. You must be available to work during normal business hours. Check out their website CVA for more info on what they do. Pay is $10 hourly. Get paid every other week via mailed check.

63. **Contract Testing Inc.** - (CTI) has been in business since 1985. They offer consumers an opportunity to do onsite studies/surveys, focus groups, take home surveys, and online studies/surveys. They offer cash incentives in exchange for your time.

64. Coupon Chief - Coupon Chief is a way to earn money by uploading the coupon codes you find. When someone uses one of your coupons to make their purchase at a participating website, the transaction will be reported to your account usually only within a few days. After a 30-day holding period and after requesting payment, you can be paid via check.

65. CopyPress - For budding copywriters, editors, designers and developers, Copy Press is a solid content mill to get you started. Users don't have to bid on freelance jobs. They can accept or decline projects as they flow in. The system is straightforward and the training materials are more than enough to get you started in the right direction.

66. Covance - Hires people in the US, Canada, and Europe to be home-based clinical research associates. Visit the jobs database and search "home-based" to find the home jobs. They also have a clinical trials page that pays pretty well if you're interested in participating in a study.

67. CreationRewards - Another fun cashback site where not only you can earn points for shopping, but you can also take surveys, answer trivia, play games, etc. They have lots of activities on the site to earn some extra cash.

68. Create My Cookbook - Have you ever wanted to create and publish a cookbook? Create my cookbook gives you all the tools you need to create a ready to publish cookbook. They do charge a fee for the finished product but it's affordable and I like that the site caters to just cookbooks and the formats are specifically for this niche. They do most of the work and you can use their platform to sell your finished product. Signup using my referral code 95LC2KTR and get $5 off

69. Create My Tattoo - You can turn your artistic abilities into a full blown business with Sign up to design custom tattoos online and get paid a 75% commission on every sale! 100% free to join and no limit to the amount of work you can submit.

70. Crowdtap - While Crowdtap doesn't seem to have as much of a focus on product testing as it used to, they still do occasionally have opportunities for you to get in on testing some products. Once you join, you'll get opportunities to answer questions and earn rewards like gift cards. Sometimes the questions you answer will lead into an invitation to test products.

71. Decluttr - Use Decluttr to get rid of your used CD's, DVD's, Blu-Ray's, and games. You can either enter there barcode for your item on their website to see an instant offer, or you can download the Decluttr app to scan the barcodes to see how much your product is worth.

72. Decorist - Work at home as an interior designer for Decorist. Build your design portfolio, Build your brand, and get paid for all your design time. You can also earn rewards through their incentive program.

73. Deed Collector - You're hired as an independent contractor to visit courthouses and collect information. They pay per accurate record submitted, not hourly. The faster you type, the more you earn. Most of their researchers average the equivalent of $15-$20/hour. They keep an updated listing on their site of what areas they are currently hiring for so check back often.

74. **Dolly** - With Dolly you can Use your truck, trailer, or just your hands to earn extra cash working whenever you choose. You can make $15 to $30 per hr. They are located in over 12 Major cities with more being added so check back often if your area is not listed.

75. **DoNow Research** - Donow research is another oldie but goodie. Not much action from them lately, but when they do have a survey or focus group that if you qualify for, you will get paid cash.

76. **DoorDash** - Get paid to pick up food orders from various restaurants that use the DoorDash service and deliver it to the people who ordered. A great way to be your own boss and set you own schedule.

77. **DreamsTime** - Upload your photos to Dreamstime and you can get 50 to 80% from each image sold. They are looking for well-defined commercial concepts. Photographers can request payment as soon as their earnings balance is $100 or more. Payments can be sent as checks, PayPal, Payoneer, or Skrill (MoneyBookers).

78. **Eatstreet** - This is a food delivery service that is different from some of the others mentioned here because they hire full time employees rather than independent contractors. Wages can be up to $17.00 an hour but keep in mind that your shift scheduling may not be quite as flexible as some of the other services. They are only hiring in specific US cities and states.

79. **Eezy** - This Company is looking for digital artists. The content they are currently seeking is Icons, Vector Illustrations, Stock Footage, and Photoshop Brushes. Upload your work and Start Earning Money. Their site states that the pay rate it is very competitive and the process to get started is fast and easy.

80. **Ebay** - Sell anything. You can set up auctions or you can give your items the "Buy It Now" option so your buyers don't have to bother with bidding. The only issue I have with Ebay (outside of their fees), is the market is over saturated. You really have to have a unique niche to sell successfully on Ebay.

81. **Ebay Partner Network** - Similar to **Amazon Associates** and **Target Affiliate Program** Ebay has a partner network that pays you a percentage from the sales you send their way. It would be a smart move to sign up because it's a big platform with thousands of products.

82. **Emerge BPO** – Hires Customer Service Advisors to work from home. A high school diploma is required. Currently hiring in Florida Georgia, Illinois, Michigan, Tennessee, and Virginia. Under the Careers tab search for "Remote".

83. **Epoll** - An online paid survey company that allows you to earn valuable reward points that can be cashed in for gift cards. I have been with them since they started and I truly have no complaints. The surveys are short and easy to qualify for.

84. **Equivity** – Hires work at home VA's with bachelor's degrees. Only a laptop and smartphone are needed. Previous experience as an executive assistant or administrative assistant a plus. U.S. based.

85. **E-Research** Incorporated in 2003, this online market research company offers you the opportunity to get paid cash payments via PayPal for your participation. Payouts start at just $2 so you can get rewarded rather quickly.

86. **E-Rewards** This one is easily on my top ten lists when it comes to paid survey companies. You get rewarded in points that can be exchanged for gift certificates or discounts. I have cashed out a lot over the years and they always have opportunities for you to earn more.

87. **EScribers** – This is a company that is frequently looking for remote legal transcribers. Experience needed. Payout is weekly.

88. **Etsy** I can't say enough good things about Etsy! I personally have an Etsy shop where I sale Antiques and Collectibles. I started in 2016 and made my first sale about two days after I opened my shop. Definitely worth looking into and it's free to join.

89. **ETutorWorld** – Openings for sales partners. You'll be selling and promoting their online courses in Math and Science. No up-front investments required. Set your own schedule. Pay is performance based.

90. **Facebook Marketplace** – Sell your stuff on Facebook and share your listings. Similar to amazon associates. You receive a commission if your audience purchases a product on Ebay using your unique link.

91. **Fancy Hands** – US only. Pay is per task and I've seen where some people claim they make anywhere from $2 to $10 an hour just depending on what tasks they choose. Pay is every other week on Tuesdays via Dwolla.

92. **Favor Delivery** - This is a pickup service operating in different areas of Texas that relies on a phone app to connect customers to drivers, and the job is basically like working as a personal assistant. You'll be sent out on errands, picking up all sorts of things for clients. The website mentions food, groceries, and dry-cleaning as common examples. This could be an interesting job in the sense that there would be a lot of variety from day to day, and the pay is decent – between 10 and 18 dollars per hour, plus tips.

93. **Field Agent** – Complete short tasks that come through on your smartphone. Get paid via direct deposit or Dwolla. The jobs generally pay $2 to $12. You won't make good money with this one but it's a fun way to make some spending money in your spare time.

94. **First Future** – ESL Teachers. Available anywhere in the US. Bachelor's degree in any subject required, as well as a high level of proficiency in English. 1 year of teaching experience is ideal (TEFL/TESOL/CELTA certificate preferred), but not required. You'll need a stable internet connection, as well as a webcam & headset. Pay is $15 – $20 / hour.

95. **Fiverr** - Fiverr is an online marketplace for freelance services. You list your skill set and set your price for your services. Jobs start at $5 (Thus the name) and can go as high as you like. For example, I do proofreading and utilize this site to solicit clients.

96. **Fleetsmith** – Customer support specialist. US. Technology oriented. 2 years' experience in customer support of a technical product via Zendesk ticketing. No phone or chat required. Full benefits package. Salary is not listed except to say that it is "competitive".

97. **FlexJobs** - FlexJobs has the marketing backing of some big-name players, like The Wall Street Journal, Forbes, NBC, and Time Magazine. Keep in mind FlexJobs is not a free site. The fee is small — just $14.95 a month without the promo code. So, this is not an expensive site to join.

98. **Foap** – Sell your iPhone images and split the profits with Foap. When anyone purchases a video or picture from your online Foap portfolio, they share the profit with you 50/50. Pays with PayPal once per month, but you must request cash out to get paid.

99. **FocusPointeGlobal** - With over 1.6 million panelists, this one is one of the biggest market research companies out there. Participate in a paid focus group, test new products, taste new snacks and beverages, watch new TV shows, take online surveys, and more!

100. **Fotolia** - 50% for each picture downloaded. You must be at least 18 years of age and the sole owner of every file you upload for sale. Every time someone purchases your content, you get a 33% commission for photos and vector art and a 35% commission for videos based on the price of the image. You can request a payout via PayPal or Skrill when you have reached at least $25 in royalties.

101. **Freelance Moms** – They want articles written for mothers who work as freelancers, focusing on actionable tips and in-depth advice. You submit an article for review, and if it is accepted you get paid $75 to $100 dollars via PayPal for your efforts.

102. **Fundrise** – If you've ever thought about investing in real-estate but you do not have the funding, Fundrise is a great place to start. The minimum investment is $500 and the return rate is pretty awesome. Check them out!!

103. **GabbyVille** – They hire home-based virtual receptionists. However, the job info is not pasted on their home page. If you are interested in working for them, you can send a cover letter and resume to career@gabbyville.com.

104. **Gametime** – Fan happiness associates to provide customer support for ticket purchasing. US. Full time, with both day and evening shifts available. Customer service experience preferred but not required. Bilingual a plus. $15 per hour and full benefits package.

105. **Gazelle** - Exchange your old cell phones and electronics for much-needed money. You'll get paid By Amazon Gift Card, PayPal or check.

106. **Getaround** - If you own a car that you don't drive very much, Getaround will pay you to rent it out to others. They will pay you monthly and claim it's possible to earn thousands per year for sharing your parked car with others. You download their app to manage the rentals. It's entirely up to you when to make your car available for rent. As of now, Getaround is primarily looking for car owners in larger metropolitan areas where there is more of a need for this service. Primary cities include Boston, Chicago, Washington, D.C., Los Angeles, New Jersey, Portland, Seattle, and San Francisco.

107. <u>Get Bellhops</u> – Drivers and movers can submit your availability in their app. They offer a simple weekly payment structure and runs average less than 15 miles. Drivers with Bellhops do not assist with loading or unloading items. Earn an average $21 an hour, including tips and bonuses. Get paid weekly, and receive extra compensation for referrals and great performance.

108. <u>Gifthulk</u> - This is a much newer site, but it has proven to be a trustworthy. Answer surveys, watch videos, play games and search the web to earn Hulk coins, and then redeem them for gift cards to your favorite retailers like Walmart, Amazon, Steam or PayPal Cash.

109. <u>Gigster</u> - They offers freelance work for designers, developers and product managers through its talent network. Projects range from wireframes and mockups to full designs. Compensation is based on the complexity of the projects

110. <u>Ginger.io</u> – Work at home as a "listener" for people who call needing to talk. Must have counseling/therapy experience. Open to US. Contract jobs that will require a degree in a related field. You work at home providing mental health services to people who need it via chat.

111. <u>GlamSquad</u> – Offering in-home makeup and beauty services. We are seeking talented hair, makeup and nail professionals to join our SQUAD Guided by collaboration, we provide customers with truly personalized experiences, in the comfort of their own homes.

112. <u>GMR Transcription</u> – This company does medical as well as other types of transcription. You can get in with no experience but you have to pass a test. Hiring from US & Canada only.

113. <u>Google Adsense</u> - Adsense is a PPC (pay per click) platform that allows you to place ads on your site and generate income based on (Clicks). Some platforms such as <u>Youtube</u> are in partnership with Adsense. You will be paid via check or direct deposit once you have accumulated $100.

114. <u>Groupon Partner</u> - Groupon is not only a great place to score big discounts, they also have an affiliate program that pays you a percentage of sales. Send traffic to their website from your platform and start earning commission today!

115. <u>Grubhub</u> - Another food delivery company focused exclusively on bringing people orders from restaurants. The website claims they get more business than other comparable services; plus you get to keep all your tips. As of now, Grubhub is only operating in larger metropolitan areas.

116. <u>Genius</u> - Lyric Transcribers. Worldwide. Only requirements are ability to work with tight deadlines and comfort using spreadsheets. Fluency in a foreign language (especially Spanish or Korean) is a big plus, but not required. Salary is unknown. No jobs available at this time but you can become a contributor.

117. <u>Guru</u> - Guru runs on a bidding system. An employer needs a document translated into French? Bid on it. Someone needs a logo for their cooking blog? Bid on it. An entrepreneur needs a ghostwriter for her new thought leadership book? You get the idea... Alternatively, companies can reach out to you directly if they search your listed area of expertise

118. **HandyPro** – If you're good with your hands you should defiantly offer handyman services. Not much information on site about the contract but they do have a lot of info on franchising.

119. **HelloTech**– Listed as a fun and flexible way to earn money on your own time. In-home tech support gigs. Jobs are paid on a per-service basis. Payouts can range from $30-$90+, depending on the level of difficulty. They submit payouts twice a week, via PayPal.

120. **Hilton** – Part time Sales and Customer Service Reps. Hiring in most states. Must have three years prior sales or customer service experience, as well as a speedy internet connection and flexible schedule. Pay unspecified, but according to Indeed.com, should be around $11-$12 / hour plus incentive and bonus payments non now check often "work at home" or Remote

121. **Hire A Helper** – Hire a Helper is mover marketplace. Visitors come to see your company reviews, prices, and credentials, then book you for your service. You only get contacted when the job is in the bag. Listing your services on this site is free and they have a network in all 50 states.

122. **HNB Naturals** – I do not promote a lot of MLM companies but Heart and Body has products that I use and find very affordable and beneficial. You get the unique opportunity to start your own Legit CBD business for FREE today! You'll have access to Pure Full Spectrum Hemp Products.

123. **Homeschool.com** – This is a great resource for those interested in homeschooling and they also select families for product testing. Testers are selected randomly, based on geography, age of children, etc. Not every family will be selected.

124. **Hubpages** – Hub Pages is a network of sites where people write about their passions and earn ongoing revenue share for publishing hubs through Adsense, Kontera, and Amazon.

125. **Hyena Cart** - Hyena Cart is another big marketplace for handmade items. They do not charge for listing items, you do have to pay $5 a month for your store but only if your store is active. You can sell earth, child, and family friendly items there. While selling handmade items is encouraged, you can also sell manufactured items that you no longer need or want.

126. **Idplr** - At Idplr you can get Free eBooks with various licenses; resell rights, master resell rights, private label rights, giveaway rights and for personal use. With a wide variety of topics, this is a great way to get your feet wet by publishing an E-book that already has all the content ready for your use.

127. **In-Home Product Testing** – when you successfully qualify and test products, IHPT provides you with an incentive for your participation in the form of an online gift card. At the successful conclusion of each IHPT survey, you will be awarded a set number of rewards points (each 1 point, will be worth $1), which can then be used to purchase online gift cards.

128. **Impact Interview** – Work at home anywhere in the US as an interview coach and help people ace their job interviews. Impact Interview is looking to add interview coaches and marketers to their team. Check Them Out.

129. Inbox Dollars - This site has quickly become a favorite in the online workers community. The signup process is quick and you can get started right away. There are plenty of opportunities to make some extra cash and they pay you out once you reach $30.

130. Independence University – Admissions Consultants. You can be located anywhere in the US. You must have a quiet work space with a speedy, wired internet connection. Degree preferred, or 4 years comparable experience in sales. Pay is around $28 / hour.

131. InfoBarrel - Make available your content (can be articles, videos, reviews, and how-to guides) and make money. You will generate revenue from your articles, and begin building a long term passive income stream.

132. InfoCision – Work from home Call Center Reps. Positions are available in AL, GA, IN, KY, NC, OJ, PA, TX & WV. Must have a Windows PC, wired internet connection and a landline phone. This is an entry level position and pay may be only around $9 – $10 / hour.

133. Information Technologies - They are interested in Independent Contractors to do courthouse research & data collecting across the nation. Pay is based on number of records collected. They do ask what experience you have in the field.

134. Innovative Network - This Company is searching for Panel Members. Passive income but they offer $10 for completing your first month plus up to $10 per survey. Check them out!!

135. Intelichek – Phone mystery shopping, call different businesses and ask questions. You will be paid monthly via direct deposit or PayPal.

136. Instacart - This Company strictly focuses on grocery delivery. Customers create a grocery list using their smart-phone app, and then you go do the shopping for them and deliver everything to their door. You set your own hours, and they pay on a weekly basis.

137. InStyle Trendsetters – You'll have insider opportunities to evaluate brand-new products, and even give us feedback about InStyle itself. They do not hit you up often but signup is fast, easy, and free so it's worth it.

138. Intuit – Become a work at home tax advisor for Intuit. Help support the Turbo Tax products over the phone. To Apply, Do a search for "remote" in the job keyword box to find the work from home listings, Most are seasonal positions so check back often.

139. I-Say Ipsos - will reward you with PayPal cash, Visa debit cards, or gift cards to various retailers once you cash out from taking surveys. You need at least 500 points in your account to redeem for anything. If you attempt a survey and do not qualify, Ipsos will still give you 5 points for your time spent.

140. ISoftStone – Various independent contractor positions. Search Engine Evaluation, IT Jobs Etc. The online application process is easy and they only require you to commit to 10 hrs. Min/25 hrs. Max per week. Get paid once a month with PayPal or direct deposit.

141. **IStockPhoto** - You get 20% of the total price for images between $1 to $20 and 40% if you sell your images only on their site.

142. **IT-Boss Research** - Hires independent contractors to become court researchers for their clients. Their site states that researchers earn between $10 and $25 hourly. They have been around since 1991 and the application process is short and of course free

143. **JBS** - This Company focuses on court research but they do offer other work at home opportunities. You'd be an Independent Contractor and pay is based on records pulled not per hour. You can pull records whenever you want and no experience is needed. They have been around since 1996 with a proven track record.

144. **Jury Test Networks** - If you sign up as a juror on Jury Test, you get to review summaries of legal cases and provide feedback to the lawyers about their cases. You will get paid to do it, usually about $10.00 per case.

145. **KHM Travel Group** - Become an independent travel agent with KHM Travel Group. They do charge a monthly/Annual fee but they give you all the tools you need to run a successful travel agency from home. You must be a U.S. citizen living in the U.S. with a current and valid driver's license or state ID in order to become an agent.

146. **Kindle Direct Publishing** - If you've always wanted to write a book and didn't know where to start, Kindle Direct Publishing is the answer to your prayers. It's totally free and gives you all the tools you need to self-publish. From cover design to pricing, you get all the tools you need to be a successful author.

147. **Linkshare** - LS has been voted the #1 Affiliate Marketing Network for 8 consecutive years. They are another big network very similar to Commission Junction with hundreds of offers. They have been around since 1996 and have a really good track record. Their payout minimum is $50.

148. **Lionbridge** – Anywhere in the US. You'll need experience using Gmail, a speedy internet connection and a smartphone (Android 4.1 or higher / iPhone 4S or higher). They have several work at home jobs listed that might be of interest so it's worth checking out.

149. **Listia** – This site works fairly similar to Ebay. The big difference is that your sales give you store credits that you can use to bid on other items. You can also have the credits converted to cash if you prefer.

150. **LiveOps** - Insurance Claims Representatives. You can live anywhere in the US. You must be able to work a minimum of 45 hours per month (including weekends). Pay is based on how much time is spent talking to and assisting customers directly, so you will earn more by working during peak hours.

151. **L'Oréal USA** - L'Oréal USA Consumer Participation Panel offers you an opportunity to test products for them at home. They mail the product to you and you fill out an online questionnaire about your experience. You get to keep the products so it's a pretty fair exchange. Sign up is easy and the send out invitations often. They also have onsite opportunities that they post periodically.

152. Lugg - Earn money with your truck. If you don't own a truck you can make money as a helper. Their site states you can make up to $2.5k/week! You can set your own schedule and work when you want. You also can get paid at the end of each day via a direct deposit to your bank account.

153. Lyft – Looking for drivers nationwide. Not work at home, but very flexible. Make money on your own time giving rides to people who use the Lyft app. you are basically acting as a "personal taxi" to people who need rides in your area. Lyft has some unique earning opportunities, such as higher pay rates for "power zones" which are areas on the map where they're expecting a higher volume of ride requests.

154. Magic Ears - Earn $18-26/hr. working at home or from anywhere with a strong internet connection while taking advantage of flexible schedules, guaranteed bookings, and free professional development resources. Magic Ears handles all of the curriculum, scheduling, and parent communication, so you can focus on creating memorable learning experiences. You must have a bachelor's degree or current college enrollment to apply.

155. Mandy - This website is purely for freelance professionals in the film industry. As someone who has a background that's heavy on the entertainment side, this website seems like a dream come true! so you'll need to make sure that your portfolio is polished and current. Get access to the latest Acting auditions, Film jobs, TV Production and Stage jobs, Voiceover work, Auditions for dancers & singers, jobs in Music, Child Acting auditions and casting calls for extra's...

156. Market Force – This is one of the most popular of all the mystery shopping companies. As a Market Force mystery shopper, you'll get paid to eat and shop for free at your favorite brands. In return for your work, you'll receive a shopper payment and/or a reimbursement for free purchases or meals.

157. Maxim Health Information – Will hire coders to work from home that have three years' experience as well as certification. There are often other remote positions listed so check back often. If you type remote in the keyword field, you'll see available positions.

158. Microsoft Rewards - The payout from this program is not impressive but if you're using the platform you might as well get paid. Search, shop, or play with Microsoft and earn points that you can redeem for gift cards, sweepstakes entries, nonprofit donations, and more.

159. Micro Workers - Micro workers is a unique site that offers you a chance to earn money by doing micro jobs. It could range from $1 for taking a phone call to $5 for downloading an app. You will not make a large amount of money here but on slow days I log in and complete a few task. It's easy, interesting, and best of all free!

160. Mindfield Online - Since 2004, Mindfield Online has been connecting consumers to products and services. You can become a paid online panel member for free. They send out frequent survey invitations and you can cash out once you make at least $5

161. **Mindojo** – Content Writers. Must have experience in teaching/instruction (any subject) OR in educational content development. You'll also need perfect written / verbal English, and the ability to work at least 30 hours per week. Pay should be around $13 – $16 / hour.

162. **MLM Gateway** - I'm personally not big on MLM (Multi-Level Marketing). I do however like to keep my options open and network with others in online marketing. MLM gateway has become a great source of information and lead generation for me. If you've ever wanted to venture into MLM, this is a good place to start. It's free to join and you'll meet some pros in the field.

163. **My Points** - This one has been around since 1996. You earn Points by Shopping online, taking surveys, watching videos, reading email and more. The points can be redeemed for gift cards, travel miles or cash via PayPal. I've personally cashed out over and over again from my points for over 20yrs.

164. **My Soap Box** - My Soapbox is an online market research company. In exchange for your feedback you will earn points that can be redeemed for gift cards. You need to earn an initial 25,000 points to start redeeming for prizes and prizes cost a minimum 5,000 points. If you are actively participating the points add up fast.

165. **Mystery.org** - Customer Experience Specialists. Anywhere in the US (shift is Pacific Time). 2+ years of customer service experience and strong communication skills required, as well as experience using CRMs. pay should be around $19 / hour.

166. **MTurk** - Amazon Mechanical Turk (MTurk) is a crowdsourcing marketplace where individuals and businesses come to outsource jobs. It's much like Micro workers. There are odd jobs and assignments listed for a set amount of compensation. The jobs typically do not pay much, but it only takes a few minutes to complete and it adds up over time.

167. **Net Transcripts** – This Company is looking for Law Enforcement/Criminal Transcriptionists and Insurance Transcriptionist. You must have a high speed Internet connection, demonstrate strong computer literacy and be proficient with MS Word, and be able to proficiently use Search Engines, a Web browser and email.

168. **On Source** – Get paid to do inspections on vehicles and other property for insurance companies. You will use the On Source Inspector app to capture photos and video of vehicles and other types of property for insurance policyholders. You'll receive $18.00 per inspection plus mileage reimbursement. A background check is required.

169. **Opinion Bar** - In business since early 1999, Opinion Bar invites its members by email for paid surveys. They pay between 1.00 and 10.00 USD for each survey you complete. They also we will invite you to test products at home.

170. **Opinion Square** - This Internet research panel has over 2 million members. You can install software which tracks Internet activity and earn points redeemable for prizes and gift cards. You can also take surveys. I cash out for Walmart gift cards often.

171. <u>Outside Agents</u> - Outside Agents is an online Travel Agent training and support company. Out of all the companies I researched, they seem to be the most affordable. They have two options. One for $21 per mo. and an unlimited package for $41 mo. They offer lots of support and pretty much all the tools you need to get up and running.

172. <u>Pinchme</u> - Sign to up to receive free samples to try. What they have changes frequently and samples have been going fast, so you'll need to be quick. I've received many samples from them and all I have to do in exchange is give a review

173. <u>Pinterest</u> - You can make money with Pinterest using Adsense or Media vine, you can also make money on Pinterest using affiliate links. Check out my resource section for a link to an article that goes more in-depth on monetizing Pinterest.

174. <u>Playtest cloud</u> – They send games to your email address. All you have to do is think out loud while you play and you'll get PayPal. If you already play games online this is an easy way to make some extra cash daily.

175. <u>Postmates</u> – Delivery Drivers. Not work at home, but you can work whenever you want to. Take home 100 percent of what you earn every time you make a delivery. They deposit your earning weekly, or you can simply cash out your earnings anytime you want. It's free to sign up and fast to get started.

176. <u>Ripple Street</u> – Sign up to do house parties with friends/family where brands send you their products for your entire group to try. This site was formerly known as House Party. I've personally hosted several parties and the party packs are always filled with great goodies. They also usually give you a gift card or coupons for free products to help your part be a success.

177. <u>Shareasale</u> - This is another Affiliate Marketing company that pays you commission based on sales you generate on your website. They work with some big name merchants and have been in business for 19yrs.

178. <u>Shipt</u> - Personal shoppers. Not work at home, but a very flexible work-when-you-want job. They claim you can earn $22 hourly or possibly more as a personal shopper for their company. You will get paid weekly with via PayPal.

179. <u>Shopify</u> - Shopify is a very popular ecommerce platform used by many major, major companies. Basically they make it very simple for you to set up your business in an online shop, using your own branding, etc. You can market your business however you would like. Unlike eBay or Amazon, your products won't show up in any sort of directory. You're basically using their platform and tools to get your shop set up how you want it.

180. <u>Shutterstock</u> - Make your creativity shine at Shutterstock and watch your earnings grow. Get your work seen by the high-volume buyers who prefer Shutterstock. It's free to sell your photos and you'll earn $0.25 to $28.00 per image.

181. **Slice The Pie** - Slice the pie launched back in 2007. It slowly became the web's largest music review engine. They pay real money (via PayPal) to reviewers for each and every review you leave. Check them out!

182. **Sponsored Tweets** - One of the biggest sites of its kind where big names like Diddy get paid to tweet. Even with a small audience you can profit from unique content. So all you have to do is, Create unique content, post it and get paid.

183. **Study.Com** - This Company hires contract freelance writers to create lessons for their students. They also occasionally have video editing positions. I could not find much information on their pay scale so you might want to reach out to them before you apply.

184. **Study Pool** This is a site where you can sign up to help people with tricky homework questions. Customers list the question they're having trouble with, and provide a rough range of prices they're willing to pay. Experts are then able to bid, and the customer can pick which expert they want to hire based on a variety of factors, including customer reviews, qualifications, and price.

185. **Sweeps Advantage** - I know entering sweepstakes is not for everyone but I have to say it has been a fun and profitable journey for me. I have won trips, cash, goods, and services. It's free and easy to enter and the potential to win a great prize is real! Check it out!!

186. **Target Affiliate Program** - Yes our beloved target has an affiliate program. You earn up to 8% when people buy from your unique link. I personally switch between Amazon Affiliates and Target depending on what I feel my followers would be interested in. It's free so you have nothing to lose!

187. **The Hauser Group** - This Company has been around since the late 90's. I've been a member as a mail decoy agent for many years. Basically you sign up as an agent and mail is sent to you to inspect its condition upon arrival. They pay quarterly and getting selected depends on if they have a need for agents in your zip code. If you are not a fit, they do have some other programs you might qualify for. It's a very reliable company and a pretty much well keep secret in the online workers community.

188. **The Penny Hoarder** - The Penny Hoarder is a great online resource for money saving tips and ways to earn an extra income. I subscribe to their newsletter and the information they provide is priceless. They also offer an affiliate program where you can refer other to their newsletter and earn e-gift cards. Take advantage of their free service and start hoarding those pennies!

189. **The Pink Panel** - As a member of this panel, you'll receive emails and Facebook posts inviting you to test exciting new products. After you try and test a product you will receive a $25 - $100 incentive in gift cards or beauty products.

190. **Top Class Actions** - I include Top class action because many consumers are not aware of the compensation they are entitled to. This site connects consumers to Lawsuits, settlements, and Attorneys. I always receive random checks in the mail, coupons for free products, and free services. They recently added a claim for cash back for anyone who purchased Ginger Ale. All you have to do is sign up for their newsletter and you can get up to date information straight to your email inbox.

191. Travel Nursing - Because there is such a high demand for qualified nurses in certain areas of the country, travel nurses typically receive more competitive wages than a full-time permanent employee. Travel nursing allows you to explore the country whether you prefer beaches to mountains or cities to small towns. They have travel assignments in all 50 states — the hardest part is deciding where to go next.

192. Tumblr - One of the most successful blogging sites ever. Although mostly used by personal bloggers, it is becoming more popular amongst serious bloggers. Tumblr is unique because it's a microblogging and social networking website combined.

193. WorkAway - The world's leading community for sustainable travel and cultural exchange. Promoting Volunteering, Family Exchanges, Homestays, Farm stays, Working Holidays, Travel Buddies, Language Learning and Cultural Exchange. This is a great way to travel in exchange for your services.

194. YouTube: You could earn money through the good old fashion Google Adsense, or you could insert your affiliate offers below your videos, though make sure that these offers can connect to your content somewhat to maximize its impact. Unique content is really the key to making real money on Youtube.

195. Ziffit.com – This Company specializes in buying book. They make the transaction process easy and fast. Payments are delivered through a variety of methods, including PayPal, bank deposit, or a check in the mail. Considering you can buy books at a thrift store or yard sale for $0.25, selling books online could turn into a very lucrative side business

Resources

99 Dollar Social will handle all your social media account for you. The offer this service for, you guessed it $99

Aliexpress – Aliexpress is a great place to get deeply discounted goods and services and offer them for resale online.

All My Tweets - View all tweets from any Twitter user on one page. Fast, Free and Easy. This site is great for viewing, searching and archiving old tweets.

Benefits.gov - The official website for information about benefits available from the U.S. government.

Coinbase - Are you interested in investing in Cryptocurrency but unsure where to start? Coinbase is hands down the best place for beginners. Signup is free and easy plus they give you multiple ways to earn FREE bitcoins!!!

Council of Non-Profits – Great info on how to start a Non-profit and related resource.

Coupon Cabin – This is a great site for online coupons and deals.

EBook Formatting – This is a great article on how to format your EBook. This site also has a resource hub for writers.

Foundation Center – This site offers tons of resources on starting a Non-profit, Grants, Training, Etc.

Franchisegator - A great online resource to discover franchises & business opportunities.

Funded – Funded offers lots of resources in areas of Angel Investors, Venture Capital, Private Equity, Investors, and Lenders.

GoDaddy – A great affordable one stop shop for your online presence. Buy your domain and have your site up and running in less than an hour.

GoFundMe - This is the largest and most popular for-profit crowdfunding platform that allows people to raise money for events and causes.

Grammarly – A must have resource for any writer. Grammarly will correct errors in grammar, spelling, style, and tone. You can use it on all platforms and It's Free!!

Grants.gov – Official site for searching and applying for government grants.

Groupon – One of the best marketplaces for connecting consumers and businesses to discounted goods and services.

Ifttt - IFTTT is an easy way to automate tasks that might otherwise be repetitive and a nice free way to get your apps and devices working together.

Jaaxy - Jaaxy is going to allow you to "spy" on your competition and probe into WHY their websites are ranking, where they are ranking.

MBDA - The Minority Business Development provides support, resources, and funding for minority-owned businesses.

Meet Libby – Meet Libby allows you to utilize your local library from the comfort of your home.

Monster Funder - This is another site like GoFundMe that allows you to set up a campaign for donations.

Notary - This site offers resources on how to become a notary. I want to stress that they do charge fees but the basic package includes the Notary stamp.

Pinterest Income – This is a really great article on how to make money using Pinterest.

The Penny Hoarder – A great online blog for tips and tricks for everything financial.

Preppr - Preppr is growing a community of like-minded Instagrammers. There are lots of resources for social media influencers.

Print-on-demand - There are so many places to make money selling T-shirts and personalized items. This article breaks it down for you and rates the best sites out there.

Robinhood – Robinhood has quickly become the favorite platform for beginners to invest in stocks.

SafeServe – If you're interested in catering or working with food in any capacity then Safe Serve certification is a must.

SBA – This is the official Government site for support and funding of Small Businesses.

Social Mobe –This is an excellent resource to schedule and track all your viral content in one place.

Stripe – Stripe offers online payment processing for internet businesses.

Tech Crunch – This is a great site for info on the startup companies.

USPS – From the comfort of your home you can schedule a package pickup, order free packing supplies, and so much more!!

Yoast - Yoast offers free tips on SEO (Search Engine Optimization). They have a free course that I highly recommend.

Wix – Wix is great site to get a free blog up and running. They offer a Fast and easy setup with lots of support and resource.

WordPress - If you're interested in starting a blog or launching a website, Wordpress is at the top of the list of places to start. They also are really affordable. Personal sites start at just $4/mo.

Recommended Reading

As a Man Thinketh by James Allen

Becoming by Michelle Obama

The 7 Habits of Highly Effective People by Stephen R. Covey

The Alchemist by Paulo Coelho

The Four Agreements by Don Miguel Ruiz

The Power of Now by Eckert Tolle

Think and Grow Rich by Napoleon Hill

When the Miracle Drops by Jesseca Dupart

About the Author

Latrice has been involved in internet marketing for over 20 years. She is also a Healthcare worker, Freelance writer, Antique Collector, and Chef. Actively involved in her community, Latrice has a passion for helping others reach their greatest potential. A native of Chicago, IL, Latrice is a mother of 4 and Grandmother of 5 who loves to travel and network. If you have any questions or concerns please contact Latrice at either email address listed below.

Email Me

Latrice.jones@yahoo.com

latricejo@gmail.com

Follow me on Social Media

Facebook @Latrice Handy Jones

Instagram @iamtricejones

Linkedin

Twitter @msjones69